MW00723505

Shadows in the Garden

PAMELA RUSHBY

Illustrated by Kevin Burgemeestre

Triple3Play

Published by
Sundance Publishing
P.O. Box 1326
234 Taylor Street
Littleton, MA 01460

Copyright © text Pamela Rushby 1999
Copyright © illustrations Kevin Burgemeestre 1999

First published 1999 as Supa Dazzlers by
Addison Wesley Longman Australia Pty Limited
95 Coventry Street
South Melbourne 3205 Australia
Exclusive United States Distribution: Sundance Publishing

ISBN 0-7608-4799-1

Printed in Canada

Contents

Chapter 1
The Tall Wooden Fence 5

Chapter 2
Old Man Watling 11

Chapter 3
A Ball Goes Over the Fence 14

Chapter 4
The Other Side of the Fence 19

Chapter 5
The Shadow 24

Chapter 6
The Other Shadow 32

Chapter 7
Who Called Me? 39

Chapter 8
Mr. Watling Changes His Mind 44

The Tall Wooden Fence

"Bye, Issy! Bye, Andy! See you tonight!"

The bus, full of high school kids, drove off down the street. Tom and Jenna waved. Andy and I were left standing on the sidewalk.

Summer vacation was over, and it was our first day at school in this town we'd moved to a few weeks ago. ("We" is my family: Mom and Dad; my older brother Tom, who's sixteen; my little sister Andy, who's nine; and me. I'm Isabel, and I'm thirteen.)

But this wasn't like other back-to-school days. This town was so small it didn't have a high school. High school kids went by bus to the next town. So, today, Tom was on the bus with our new friend, Jenna, and all the other high school kids. And Andy and I were going to the little local school.

Andy didn't seem to mind. But I did. Tom and I had always gone to school together. Even after he started high school, we'd always walked the same way. Now Tom had gotten on the bus with Jenna. And even though I liked Jenna, I didn't like it one bit that he was going to school with her. I felt left out, and lonely.

"We'd better go," said Andy.

"We've got lots of time," I said grumpily. I kicked a weed that was growing out of a crack in the sidewalk. Andy gave me a sideways look, but she didn't say anything.

We walked slowly down the street. Past the pizza shop, past the little library, past the police station. We went down a street of old houses with wide porches and big yards, on to another street.

This street was different. The houses here were new, and small. Their yards were very small. We knew some of the kids who lived here.

The kids from this street liked coming to play at our place, because Tom and Andy and I lived in an old house with a big yard.

There was no room to play anything in their yards, they said. Football was hopeless. Even volleyball was a problem. So the kids from this street played on some of the lots that hadn't been built on yet. A few kids were there this morning. They were kicking a soccer ball around, having a quick game before school. One of the kids we knew, Nico Manaltos, was the goalie.

Andy waved. `Over here!" she yelled. Nico kicked the ball over to Andy. I could see that those kids didn't think for a minute that Andy would be any good at soccer. Nico didn't even bother guarding the goal. But I thought Andy might surprise them. Our brother Tom is serious about soccer. Andy and I have been playing with him in the backyard for years. Andy's not bad. So when she kicked the ball just where she meant to, right into their goal, those kids looked pretty surprised. I grinned to myself.

The ball came our way again. This time Nico moved in front of the goal. "Huh!" said Andy. "You show 'em, Issy!"

All right, I thought. I will.

I took a quick run, aimed, and kicked the ball as hard as I could.

The ball shot toward the goal. Nico dived for it, but he missed. The ball hurtled on and thudded into the tall wooden fence behind the goal. The fence shook.

The kids scattered. In seconds, Andy and I were the only ones in sight.

 Old Man Watling

Andy and I looked around to see what had scared everyone. Nothing happened.

After a minute, the kids came back. They kept an eye on the fence.

"Whew!" said Nico. "He didn't hear it."

"Who didn't hear what?" I asked.

"Old man Watling. He goes ballistic if balls hit his fence. And if they go over it—look out!"

"Who's old man Watling?" asked Andy.

It was time for school. The kids started walking along with us.

"Old man Watling lives in the house behind the fence," said Nico. Andy and I looked. The wooden fence was higher than our heads, and very solid. Over the top of the fence we could see trees, and through the leaves, the roof of a house. It was a corrugated metal roof, a little rusty and very big.

"Old man Watling used to own the land our houses are built on," said Nico. "It was all part of his property. When he sold the land and the houses were built, he had that fence put up. And is he a grouch! Complains about everything! Noise, dogs, balls in his yard . . ."

There was a gate in the fence. I went up to it and tried to see through the cracks.

"Don't do that!" said the kids. They sounded really scared.

"Why not?" I asked. "I'm only looking."

"He doesn't like people looking in," said Nico. "If he sees you, he'll yell."

"Huh! Who cares?" I said. "He can't complain if you only *look*."

"Oh, yes, he can," said Nico. "C'mon, let's go!" They all ran off. Andy and I shrugged our shoulders, and ran after them. I'd come back later and have a real look, I told myself. Old man Watling didn't frighten me!

Chapter 3

A Ball Goes Over the Fence

I walked home from school by myself that afternoon. Andy had gone off with some of the kids from her class. Andy never seemed to have any trouble making friends.

I felt lonelier than ever. I'd been feeling grumpy all day, so I didn't even try to make friends. I still missed Tom.

As I passed the gate in the high fence, I paused. I really wanted to see what was inside.

I went up to the gate and peered through. I couldn't see much. The trees and bushes were so overgrown and tangled that I could barely see the big old house behind them.

"And just what are *you* doing?" said a voice behind me. I jumped. The mail carrier had walked up quietly from the house next door, and I hadn't heard her coming.

"I'm not doing anything," I said. "I'm just looking. Who lives here, anyway?"

The mail carrier pushed some mail into a slot cut in the gate. "Mr. Watling," she said.

"Does he live by himself?" I asked.

The mail carrier gave me a sharp look. "Why do you want to know?" she asked. "You can't go in there."

"I wasn't going in," I said. "It just looks interesting."

"Well, keep out," said the mail carrier. "Mr. Watling doesn't like people bothering him." She gave me another sharp look and walked off.

Wow! I thought. That mail carrier was the suspicious type. Did I look as if I was going to rob the place?

I looked through the cracks in the gate again. The garden was incredible—overgrown and jungly and shadowy. I had to admit, I wanted to go in. Still, I figured that the mail carrier was probably right. Best to keep out.

Down the street, the kids were playing soccer again.

"Hey, Isabel!" they called. "Want to play?"

I stopped. I'd been grumpy all day. I was sick of being grumpy. "OK!" I called.

Some of the kids were pretty good players—especially Nico and a little kid named Mike. Mike looked no older than eight, but he could really handle that ball. We played until it was late. Then I thought I'd better go home.

"Last kick!" shouted Mike.

He sent the ball over to me. It was high, so I headed it back to him. At least, I meant to head it back to him. But instead of going where I meant it to, the ball curved in the air. It went . . . right over Mr. Watling's fence.

Chapter 4

The Other Side of the Fence

There was dead silence. Mike looked really upset. "It was my new ball," he said.

I felt terrible. "I'm really sorry," I said.

"I know you didn't mean it," Mike said. "But I got that ball for my birthday." He turned and started to walk away.

The other kids turned to go, too. I looked at the fence. It wasn't too high.

Well, not all *that* high. I could climb it, I thought. Maybe. At least I could try!

I found a big knothole to help me up. I put my toe in it, heaved, jumped, and balanced on the top of the fence.

The kids swung around. "Old man Watling will *murder* you!" they said.

I wobbled on the top of the fence. "Only if he sees me," I said, dropping into the yard. I landed in a shadowy, overgrown garden.

I saw Mike's ball at once, but I didn't pick it up. I wanted to look around, now that I was here. So I did.

I was standing in grass up to my knees. A brick path, with moss growing between the bricks, led to the house.

Halfway down the path there was a little pond with a fountain in the middle. The fountain wasn't working, and the water in the pond was dark and slimy. Long strands of wisteria waved over my head.

A big rosebush, covered with white roses, stood near the pond. While I watched, the bush trembled, as if someone had brushed against it. But it must have been a breeze.

"But there is no breeze," I said to myself.

One white rose dropped all its petals, *plop*, onto the path. The air was so still I could hear them fall.

Mr. Watling's garden was mysterious and strange and quiet. I went a few more steps toward the house, trying to see more. And suddenly the garden wasn't quiet any more.

"Hey!" someone shouted. "You! Girl! What are you doing in here?"

Old man Watling!

I ran for it. A man was coming out of the glass door that led from the back porch of the house. He was waving a walking stick.

I snatched up Mike's ball and leaped for the
fence. I couldn't get over it, holding the ball.
I flung the ball over, jumped for the fence
again, and tumbled over the top.

"You stay out!" I heard him shout. "Don't you
ever come in here again!"

"Not a chance!" I said to myself. I had
skinned my knees and was scared out of my
wits. The kids had all scattered. I ran after
them. No way was I going in there again!

Chapter 5

The Shadow

But I did.

None of us went anywhere near the fence or the old house for a few days. But the empty lots were too tempting. The kids started playing soccer there again.

I usually joined in. Tom's school bus didn't get back to town until late in the afternoon. I had a lot of time to fill after school.

I often looked at the fence and wondered about the garden behind it. I wanted to see it again. But I said I'd never go in there again.

That's what I said, but one afternoon, I found myself hanging around on the empty lot near the fence after the other kids had gone.

I said I'd never go in there again—but I found myself swinging up on top of the fence, balancing there for a moment, and then dropping down silently into the garden.

Late in the afternoon, the garden seemed even more strange and secret. It was full of shadows. I didn't want Mr. Watling to catch me, so I kept in the shadows, creeping along from one to the next. I was almost like a shadow myself, I thought.

I grinned to myself. The Shadow—I'm The Shadow, I thought.

Nobody sees me, nobody knows where I've been. The Shadow! I liked the idea. I slid along, hiding in the half-dark, being The Shadow, watching the house.

And then I started to feel as if someone was watching *me*. I turned quickly. There was no one behind me, but the long grass was moving, as if someone had just passed by.

It's the breeze, I told myself. But there was no breeze.

It was a bit creepy. "Don't be silly!" I told myself. "There's no one here."

But suddenly I wanted to go home. I wanted to be back with Mom and Dad and Andy and Tom, in our warm, noisy, brightly lit house.

I went home. But the next afternoon, I was back in the garden.

And the next, and the next.

I didn't do anything. I didn't touch anything. I just looked at the garden and the house, as I slipped from bush to bush, like a shadow.

Each afternoon, the feeling that someone was watching me grew stronger. Often I saw plants and bushes move, as if someone had brushed by them. A couple of times, out of the corner of my eye, I thought I caught a glimpse of a green coat. And once, as I gazed into the dark water of the pond, I thought I saw another face reflected beside mine. Then the water moved, and the face was gone.

I started to think of what I saw as The Other Shadow.

Who could it be? Surely not Mr. Watling! He would have chased me. But Mr. Watling was the only person who lived here. And The Other Shadow somehow didn't seem unfriendly. I felt it didn't mind my being in the garden. It was a mystery . . . and I decided I liked mysteries.

So I went back into the garden, day after day. The garden was silent and shadowy and so beautiful. And there was only me and The Other Shadow there.

One day, I was in the garden early, right after school. The kids weren't playing soccer; instead, they were staying at school for intramural sports. But I hadn't wanted to stay. This was my chance to spend more time in the garden.

It was nice being there earlier, with the sun still high. It was bright and beautiful in the garden. Too bright for me to be The Shadow. I sat under the big rosebush and just looked around. The Other Shadow didn't seem to be around.

The sun warmed my face, and I started to feel drowsy. I closed my eyes, enjoying it. When I looked at the house again, I thought the glare from the sun was making me see things. There was a figure standing behind the glass door that led to the porch. I couldn't see the figure clearly because the glass was reflecting the light from the garden, but it seemed to be looking straight at me.

Chapter 6

The Other Shadow

My heart jumped. Mr. Watling! I thought. I
flopped down flat in the long grass. Maybe
he hadn't seen me.

When I looked again, the figure was still
there, still looking in my direction. But
now, it seemed to be beckoning to me.
Beckoning urgently.

Did Mr. Watling think I was crazy enough to
run over there to get yelled at? Not me! I got
ready to split. Then I took another look.

I caught a glimpse of green through the reflection in the glass door. The Other Shadow wore a green coat, I thought. Maybe the figure wasn't Mr. Watling at all?

The figure beckoned again, even more urgently. I hesitated. Mr. Watling wanted something. What? Should I answer? And if I answered, would I be in big trouble?

Who cares? I thought. I had to go and see what that beckoning figure wanted. Not bothering to hide now, I walked slowly up the brick path to the house. I was closer to the house than I'd ever been. I was right at the porch steps.

The figure was gone, but the glass door was wide open.

I tiptoed up the steps. No one was there. "Mr. Watling?" I called. "Is that you?" No answer.

Great! I thought. There's no one here—I'm going! But I couldn't. Someone wanted me. I felt I had to go on. I tiptoed across the porch. In the hall inside, umbrellas and hats and coats were hanging from pegs. The hall was dim, but I could see that one coat was green.

A green coat! The Other Shadow? I touched the coat gently. The feeling grew stronger that something was telling me to keep going. I went on down the hall.

I didn't like it. I wanted to go home. But something was still telling me that someone needed me.

35

"Mr. Watling?" I called again. My voice sounded funny. "Are you here?"

And this time someone answered. "Here!" a voice croaked. "I'm here!"

I ran down the hall. It opened into an entryway with stairs leading to the next floor. At the bottom of the stairs lay Mr. Watling. At least, I supposed it was Mr. Watling. He was an old man. And he had a walking stick beside him.

When he heard me coming, he tried to struggle up. He looked frightened. I suppose he didn't know who I was.

"Mr. Watling?" I said. "What's wrong? Are you sick?"

He couldn't say very much. "Phone," he croaked. "Phone!"

"Phone for help?" I asked. "The ambulance?"
Mr. Watling nodded, then he flopped back
onto the floor.

I found the phone and dialed 911. I told the operator I needed an ambulance.

"I don't know what's wrong," I said. "He beckoned to me to come into the house, and when I did, he was lying on the floor. He must have felt sick and then collapsed."

The emergency operator told me what to do, and said an ambulance would be there shortly. The operator was right. By the time I'd made sure Mr. Watling's breathing wasn't obstructed and had found a blanket and a pillow, I only had a few minutes to wait. But they seemed like very long minutes, sitting on the floor beside Mr. Watling, listening to his shallow breathing. I was really glad when the ambulance arrived.

Chapter 7

Who Called Me?

The EMTs gently checked out Mr. Watling, and then put him onto a stretcher. They carried him to the ambulance. I followed them out.

The mail carrier was coming up the path. "I saw the gate open," she said. "What's going on? Can I help?"

"We'll be all right now," said one of the EMTs from the ambulance. "Mr. Watling seems to have had an accident. Looks like he took a tumble down the stairs."

I stared at him. "Down the stairs?" I said. "But—"

"Good thing Isabel happened to drop by," said the other EMT. "I'd say he'd been lying there for a couple of hours already."

"A couple of hours?" I said. "But—"

One EMT climbed into the back of the ambulance with Mr. Watling. The other one slammed the door shut. "Good day's work, young Isabel," he said. "We'll let you know how he's getting on. But I think he'll be fine. Bye!"

"But—" I said. "But—"

They didn't hear me. They drove off down the street.

The mail carrier and I stood looking after the ambulance. Then she gave me a sharp look. "Just happened to drop by, eh?" she said.

"But he *couldn't* have been there for a few hours!" I burst out. "He called me from the back-porch door!"

"Did he really?" said the mail carrier. "Show me where."

We walked around the house together. "Just there, behind the glass door," I pointed. "He was wearing a green coat. The green coat hanging in the hall. It had to be him. It had to!" I looked at her. "Didn't it?" I asked.

The mail carrier stared at me. "I don't know who you saw," she said, "but it looks as if it wasn't Mr. Watling."

I didn't think I liked that answer. "Then *who* did I see?" I asked.

"Well," said the mail carrier slowly. "Mr. Watling lives alone now. But someone else did live here once. Someone who loved the garden and spent a lot of time in it. She often wore a green coat."

"She?" I questioned.

"Beryl Watling," she said. "Mr. Watling's wife."

"So *Mrs.* Watling called me?" I said. "It was Mrs. Watling I saw?"

"Oh, no," said the mail carrier. "You couldn't have seen Mrs. Watling." She paused. "She died over a year ago."

We looked at each other. In the garden, a little breeze sent shadows chasing across the grass.

Chapter 8

Mr. Watling Changes His Mind

Mr. Watling was home in a few days. He called and asked if I could stop by to see him. This time, I didn't climb the fence. I went in the front gate and walked right up to the front door.

Mr. Watling wanted to thank me, he said. "Lucky for me you came along. Even though you shouldn't have been in my garden!"

"Yes," I said. "I'm sorry. I won't come in again. I promise."

"Well," said Mr. Watling. "I've been thinking, and I've changed my mind. I'd like you children to use the garden. Not to play soccer, though," he said hastily. "Not near my roses! But you can use it. I'll take the lock off the gate so you can come in anytime."

"Really?" I said. "I'd love that! I think it's a beautiful garden!"

"Yes," said Mr. Watling. "Someone else thought so, too."

"I know," I said softly.

Mr. Watling sighed. "I haven't felt much like gardening lately. I'm afraid that the garden has gotten away from me."

"Um . . . Mr. Watling," I said, "could I help you clean up the garden? I'd like to do that. I like gardens."

Mr. Watling smiled. "Thanks, Isabel," he said. "That would be great."

About the Author

Pamela Rushby

Pamela Rushby has worked in advertising, as a preschool teacher, and as a freelance writer. She is currently a television writer and producer.

Pamela has written over 30 books for children. She lives with her husband, two children, a three-legged cat, and six visiting wild turkeys that peck at the back door for handouts.

She is passionately interested in children's books, television, ancient history, and Middle Eastern food. Although Pamela likes writing about ghosts, she has never met one personally.

About the Illustrator

Kevin Burgemeestre

Kevin illustrates books and prepares collages for a magazine. When he illustrates with ink, Kevin uses a dip-in mapping pen in a loose, friendly manner. For his colored illustrations, he works in either watercolor with soft washes, or strong color applied with sponges. Kevin's collages reflect his passion for movies and cubism, and sometimes end up as sculptures.

Kevin works out of his own studio, which he shares with his enormous collection of car magazines, and his young son, Jim, drawing, drawing, drawing . . .